Fahrenheit 451

Ray Bradbury

STUDENT PACKET

NOTE:

The trade book edition of the novel used to prepare this guide is found in the Novel Units catalog and on the Novel Units website. Using other editions may have varied page references.

Please note: We have assigned Interest Levels based on our knowledge of the themes and ideas of the books included in the Novel Units sets, however, please assess the appropriateness of this novel or trade book for the age level and maturity of your students prior to reading with them. You know your students best!

ISBN 978-1-56137-302-4

Printed in the United States of America.

To order, contact your local school supply store, or:

Toll-Free Fax: 877.716.7272
Phone: 888.650.4224
3901 Union Blvd., Suite 155
St. Louis, MO 63115

sales@novelunits.com

novelunits.com

Note to the Teacher

Selected activities, quizzes, and test questions in this Novel Units® Student Packet are labeled with the following reading/language arts skills for quick reference. These skills can be found above quiz/test questions or sections and in the activity headings.

Basic Understanding: The student will demonstrate a basic understanding of written texts. The student will:

- use a text's structure or other sources to locate and recall information (Locate Information)
- determine main idea and identify relevant facts and details (Main Idea and Details)
- use prior knowledge and experience to comprehend and bring meaning to a text (Prior Knowledge)
- summarize major ideas in a text (Summarize Major Ideas)

Literary Elements: The student will apply knowledge of literary elements to understand written texts. The student will:

- analyze characters from a story (Character Analysis)
- analyze conflict and problem resolution (Conflict/Resolution)
- recognize and interpret literary devices (flashback, foreshadowing, symbolism, simile, metaphor, etc.) (Literary Devices)
- consider characters' points of view (Point of View)
- recognize and analyze a story's setting (Setting)
- understand and explain themes in a text (Theme)

Analyze Written Texts: The student will use a variety of strategies to analyze written texts. The student will:

- identify the author's purpose (Author's Purpose)
- identify cause and effect relationships in a text (Cause/Effect)
- identify characteristics representative of a given genre (Genre)
- interpret information given in a text (Interpret Text)
- make and verify predictions with information from a text (Predictions)
- sequence events in chronological order (Sequencing)
- identify and use multiple text formats (Text Format)
- follow written directions and write directions for others to follow (Follow/Write Directions)

Critical Thinking: The student will apply critical-thinking skills to analyze written texts. The student will:

- write and complete analogies (Analogies)
- find similarities and differences throughout a text (Compare/Contrast)
- draw conclusions from information given (Drawing Conclusions)
- make and explain inferences (Inferences)
- respond to texts by making connections and observations (Making Connections)
- recognize and identify the mood of a text (Mood)
- recognize an author's style and how it affects a text (Style)
- support responses by referring to relevant aspects of a text (Support Responses)
- recognize and identify the author's tone (Tone)
- write to entertain, such as through humorous poetry or short stories (Write to Entertain)
- write to express ideas (Write to Express)
- write to inform (Write to Inform)
- write to persuade (Write to Persuade)
- demonstrate understanding by creating visual images based on text descriptions (Visualizing)
- practice math skills as they relate to a text (Math Skills)

Name ______________________________

Attribute Web

Directions: Use the attribute web below to brainstorm about the word "conformity," especially as it relates to society.

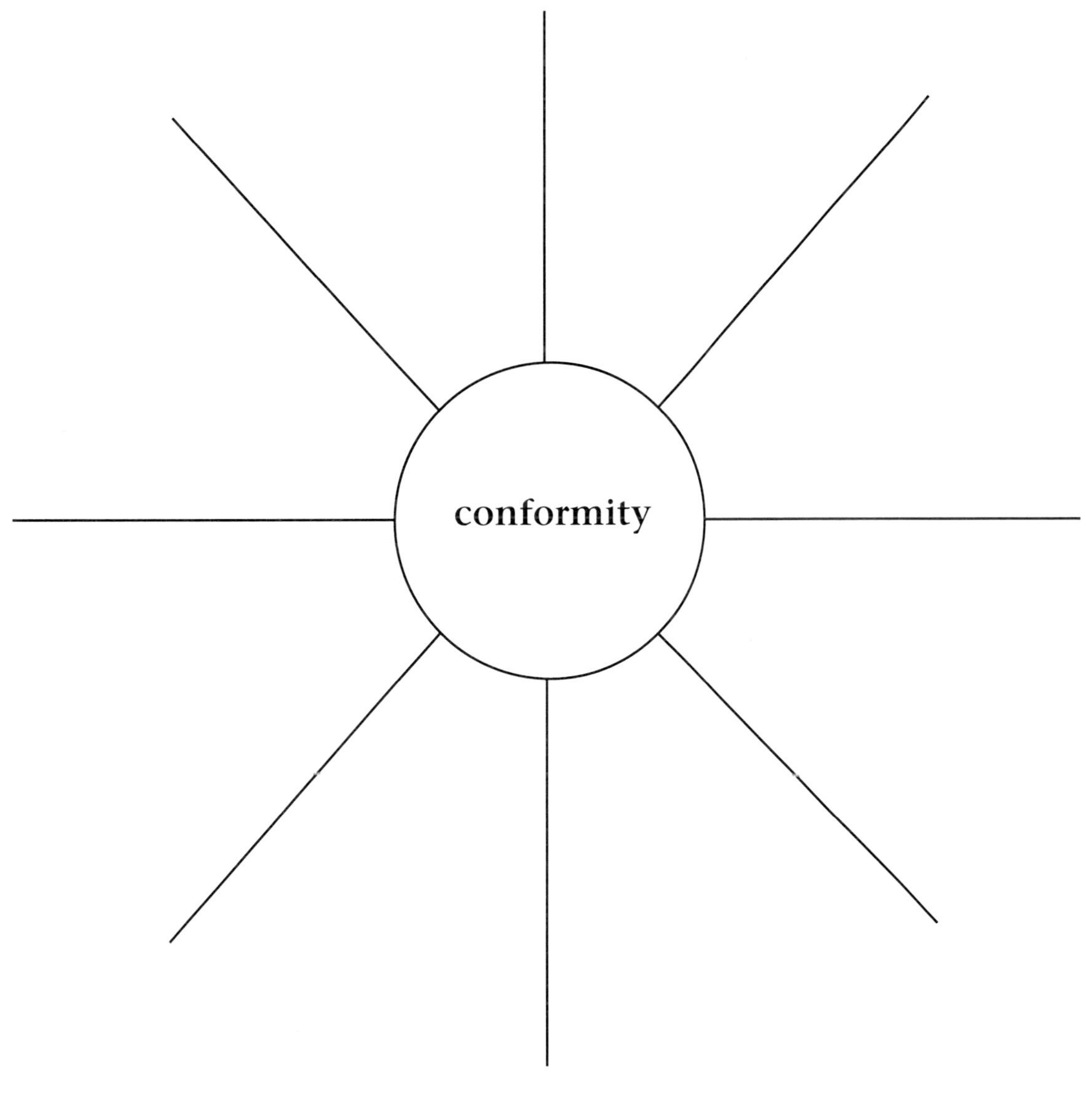

Name ______________________________

Getting the "Lay of the Land"

Directions: Prepare for reading by answering the following short-answer questions.

1. Who is the author?

   ____

2. What does the title suggest to you about the novel?

   ____
   ____
   ____
   ____

3. When was the novel first copyrighted?

   ____

4. How many pages are there in the novel?

   ____

5. Thumb through the novel. Read three pages—one from near the beginning, one from near the middle, and one from near the end. What predictions can you make about the novel?

   ____
   ____
   ____
   ____
   ____

6. What does the cover suggest to you about the novel?

   ____
   ____
   ____
   ____
   ____

Name ______________________________

Vocabulary Connections and Fill-in

venomous	stolid	minstrel	phoenix
amber	tallow	moonstones	stratum
cataract	capillary	olfactory	proboscis
multifaceted	ballistics	trajectory	

A. Directions: On the line beneath each word pair below, tell how the two words are related.

1. olfactory/proboscis

   ____

2. amber/moonstones

   ____

3. ballistics/trajectory

   ____

B. Directions: Fill in the correct vocabulary word in each sentence below.

4. In 1415, streetlights were made using ____________________, which was inexpensive since it was an animal byproduct.
5. Though popular in the 1800s, ____________________ shows declined in popularity in the twentieth century, mostly due to the advent of vaudeville acts.
6. The geologist cut deep into the cliff face to see if he could find a(n) ____________________ of stone that could tell when the rock was formed.
7. The newly engaged bride showed off her brilliant, ____________________ diamond set in a white-gold band.
8. The snake had markings that made Jeremy sure it was ____________________.
9. Jenna's uncle warned her to avoid the cacti on his ranch, since the small, ____________________ cactus needles were painful to remove from skin.
10. The bird flying over the mouth of the erupting volcano was reminiscent of a(n) ____________________ rising from ashes.
11. The judge's face was ____________________ and unmoved when he made his final ruling in the case.
12. The stray dog had a(n) ____________________ in one eye, but surgery soon restored its vision.

Name ______________________________

Vocabulary/Plot Association

rollick	luminescent	digests	resume
centrifuge	pratfall	sauterne	nomadic
cartographers	dictum	breach	memoriams
bestial	tactile		

Directions: Select four of the above vocabulary words. On the lines below, explain in two to three sentences why that word is important to the plot of *Fahrenheit 451*.

Word #1: ____________________________

____

____

____

Word #2: ____________________________

____

____

____

Word #3: ____________________________

____

____

____

Word #4: ____________________________

____

____

____

Name ______________________________

Vocabulary Word Map

exhalation	cadenced	suffused	retaliation
profusion	loam	praetorian	insidious
linguists	harlequin	welter	bobbins
complementing	contemptible		

Directions: Complete a word map like the one below for seven of the above vocabulary words.

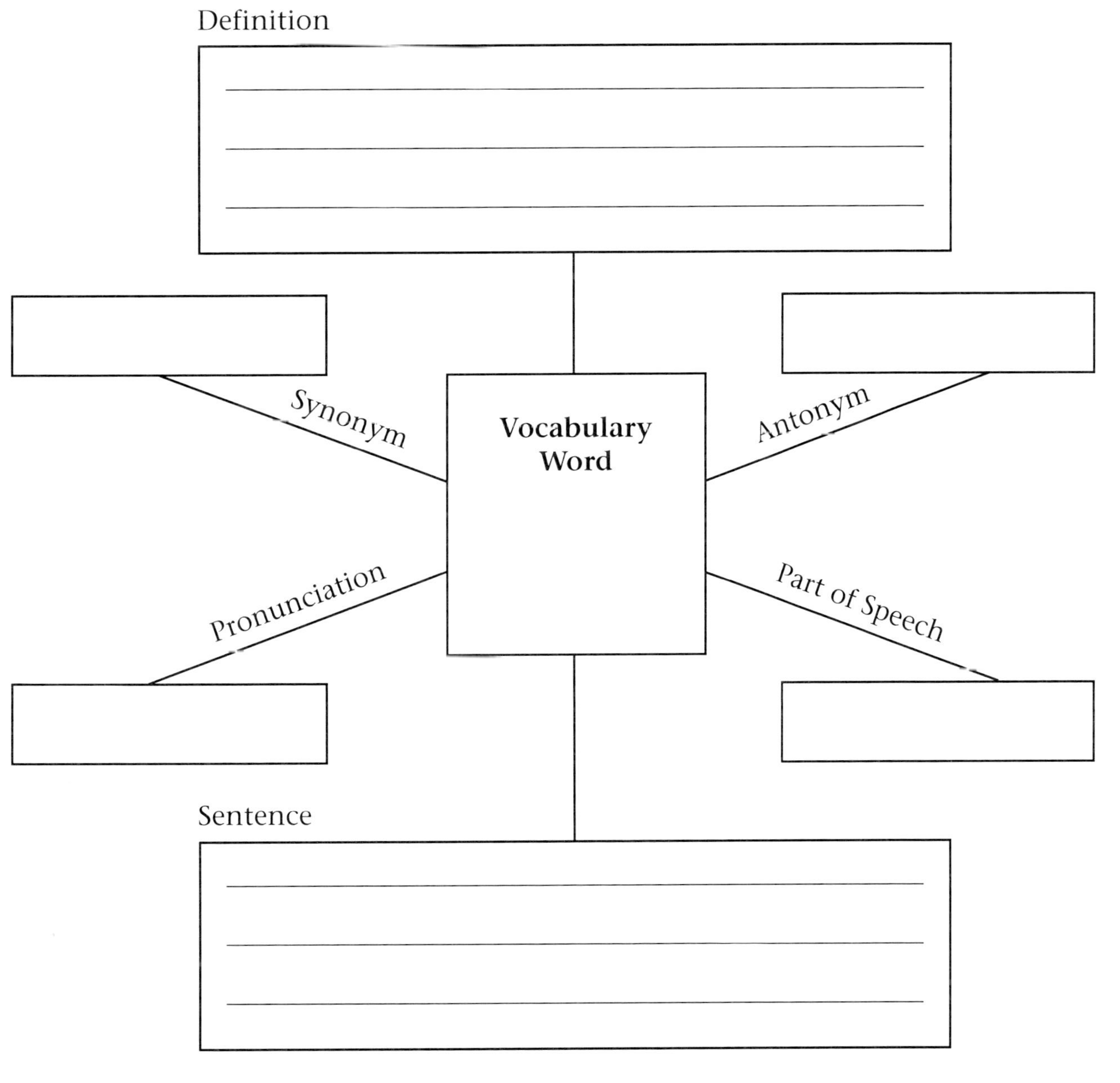

Name ______________________________

Vocabulary Elimination

contracting	ruinous	filigree	invigorated
latrine	parried	verbiage	oracle
rebut	beatific	perfunctorily	gaseous
chaff	phosphorescent		

Directions: Circle the word that does not belong in each row below.

1.	**contracting**	squeezing	tightening	overflowing	shrinking
2.	**ruinous**	damaging	jealous	destructive	harmful
3.	**filigree**	ornamental	fashionable	intricate	delicate
4.	**invigorated**	loosened	strengthened	revitalized	enlivened
5.	**latrine**	outhouse	lavatory	privy	shower
6.	**parried**	evaded	directed	escaped	deflected
7.	**verbiage**	wordiness	inadequacy	excess	repetition
8.	**oracle**	prophet	visionary	protector	seer
9.	**rebut**	separate	deny	refute	negate
10.	**beatific**	rapturous	joyful	delightful	stunning
11.	**perfunctorily**	instinctively	unconsciously	deliberately	automatically
12.	**gaseous**	vaporous	opaque	pneumatic	aerated
13.	**chaff**	disrespectful	worthless	irrelevant	insignificant
14.	**phosphorescent**	glowing	incandescent	shining	scorching

Name ______________________________

Vocabulary Crossword

incomprehensible	gout	rend	literateur
manikin	liquefaction	bole	penance
plummeting	quarry	dilate	luminous
limned	valise		

Directions: Complete the crossword puzzle below.

Across

3. trunk of a tree
5. shown in outline
7. dropping steeply and suddenly downward
9. voluntary self-punishment to show sorrow for committing a sin
14. beyond understanding

Down

1. small piece of luggage
2. emitting or reflecting light
4. process of turning into liquid
6. become wider or larger
8. person who is knowledgeable about literature
10. object of a hunt
11. form representing the human figure
12. large blob or clot of something
13. tear into multiple pieces

Name ______________________________

Vocabulary by Association

juggernaut	guild	musk	cardamom
incite	incriminate	convolutions	scythe
squanders	desolation	incessantly	oilskin
pyre	wick		

Directions: Define and associate each vocabulary word above with a character from *Fahrenheit 451*, and in the chart below, explain why that word matches your chosen character's personality. You may associate more than one word with a character, but use no more than three words per character.

Word(s)	Character	Explanation

Name ______________________________

Directions: Answer the following questions on a separate sheet of paper. Use your answers in class discussions, for writing assignments, and to review for tests.

Part One: The Hearth and the Salamander

Pages 1–29

1. What is Montag doing at the beginning of the novel?
2. Why does Montag slow as he reaches a corner near his house?
3. Describe Clarisse McClellan the first time Montag sees her.
4. What does Montag tell Clarisse is against the law?
5. What is the last question Clarisse asks Montag during their first encounter?
6. What room does Montag describe as a "cold marbled room of a mausoleum" (p. 9)?
7. What happened to Mildred?
8. What do the two machines brought in by the operators do?
9. What does Mildred usually do for most of the day?
10. What does Clarisse tell Montag about rain?
11. What does Clarisse tell Montag that the dandelion proves?
12. What does Montag refer to as "the dead beast, the living beast" (p. 22)?
13. Why does Montag think this beast dislikes him?
14. Why is Clarisse afraid of children her own age?

Pages 29–66

1. Where does Montag learn the phrase "once upon a time" (p. 31)?
2. How is the scene at Elm Street different than other alarms to which Montag has responded?
3. Who are "the relatives"?
4. What does Mildred say happened to Clarisse?
5. Why does Montag claim he became a fireman?
6. Why does Captain Beatty come to Montag's house?
7. What is printed on the lid of Beatty's eternal matchbox?
8. What does Beatty claim happened to books over the years?
9. Why is Montag agitated as Mildred tries to adjust his pillow?
10. What does Beatty say the country needs most of all?
11. What does Mildred suggest Montag do to get rid of his anger?
12. What does Montag pull out of the air conditioning vent?
13. What is Mildred's reaction to what Montag reveals?
14. What do Clarisse and the woman who burned her own house make Montag realize?

Name ______________________________

Part Two: The Sieve and the Sand

Pages 67–88

1. As Montag reads the words of famous authors, of whom is he reminded?
2. Why doesn't the doorbell sound when someone approaches the door while Montag is reading?
3. How does Mildred become willingly distracted from Montag and his books?
4. Why does Montag suddenly remember meeting a man named Faber in the park?
5. How does Montag feel as he gets on the subway?
6. To what does Montag compare himself and the words he reads in the Bible?
7. What in the subway distracts Montag from his memorization of the Bible?
8. Why does Faber say Montag is brave?
9. What three things does Faber say are now missing from the world?
10. What joking plan of Faber's does Montag take seriously?
11. How does Montag get Faber to agree to teach him?
12. What is Faber's hobby?
13. How did Faber finance his hobby?
14. What is Faber's invention?

Pages 88–106

1. Why does Montag protest to doing what Faber tells him?
2. How does Faber plan to help Montag retain knowledge?
3. What does Montag do that irritates Mildred, Mrs. Phelps, and Mrs. Bowles?
4. Why is Montag irritated when the three women begin talking about politics?
5. What does Montag do that makes Mrs. Phelps cry?
6. Why is Montag's stack of books smaller than before?
7. Where does Montag hide his books next?
8. What does Montag hand Beatty as soon as he walks into the firehouse?
9. What does Faber say is "the most dangerous enemy to truth and freedom" (p. 104)?
10. Where does the fire alarm lead the men?

Part Three: Burning Bright

Pages 107–133

1. How does Beatty say he warned Montag?
2. What does Beatty say is fire's "real beauty"?
3. Why can't Montag run away from Beatty and the firemen?
4. What does Beatty force Montag to do?
5. Who reported Montag's possession of books?
6. Why does Beatty strike Montag in the head?
7. What does Montag do to both Beatty and the Mechanical Hound?
8. What theory does Montag have about Beatty?
9. What does Montag hear on his Seashell radio?
10. In what direction does Montag realize he is running?
11. What happens to Montag as he walks on the empty boulevard?
12. What does Montag realize about the kids driving the beetle?
13. Where does Montag stop before he reaches his destination? What does he leave there, and why?
14. Why does Faber say he "feel[s] alive for the first time in years" (p. 125)?
15. What do Montag and Faber see on a news report that makes them nervous?
16. What does Montag instruct Faber to do to get rid of Montag's scent?
17. What are the people of Elm Terrace instructed to do by police?
18. How does Montag escape detection by the Hound?

Pages 133–158

1. Where does Montag imagine himself sleeping?
2. What animal does Montag mistake for the Hound?
3. What does Montag's foot hit in the darkness?
4. Of what fact is Montag certain as he follows his new path?
5. What two things do the five old men give Montag to drink?
6. How is "Montag" caught?
7. Besides Granger, who are the other four men in the circle? What were their former occupations?
8. What is Montag's literary contribution to the group?
9. Why was Granger sad when his grandfather died?
10. What happens to the city?
11. To where are the men traveling, and why?

Name ______________________________

Law-Abiding Citizens

Directions: Use the boxes below to list six attributes of a good citizen in Guy Montag's world.

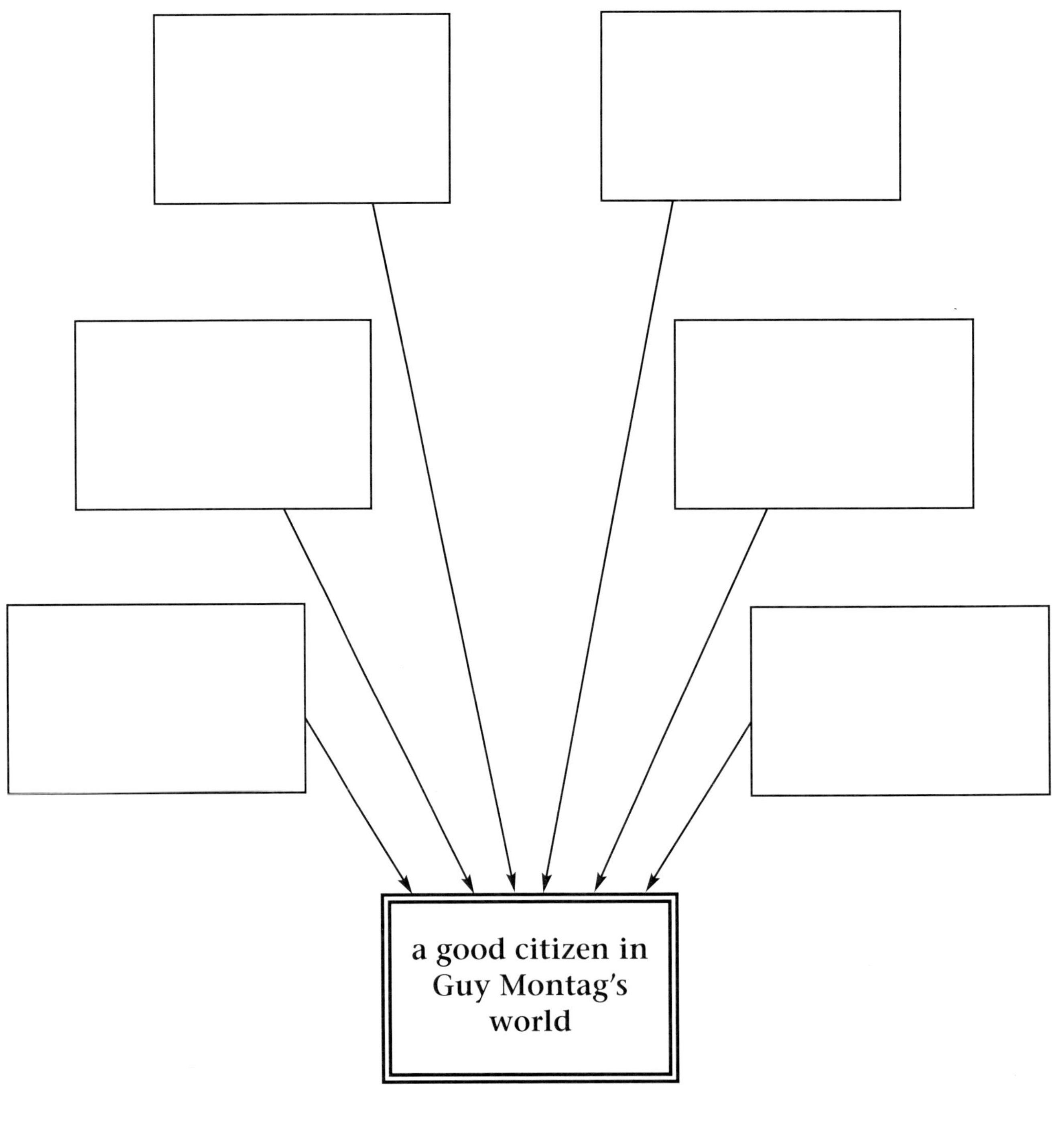

Name ______________________________

Conflict

The **conflict** of a story is the struggle between two people or two forces. There are three main types of conflict: person vs. person, person vs. nature or society, and person vs. self.

Directions: The characters experience some conflicts in the story. In the chart below, list the names of three major characters. In the space provided, list a conflict each character experiences. Then, explain how each conflict is resolved in the story.

Character:

Conflict	Resolution

Character:

Conflict	Resolution

Character:

Conflict	Resolution

Name ______________________________

Characterization

Directions: In Part One of *Fahrenheit 451,* Guy Montag begins to question his society and the life he is living. The other characters in the novel cause these changes in Montag. In the boxes below, give examples of how the characters influenced Montag.

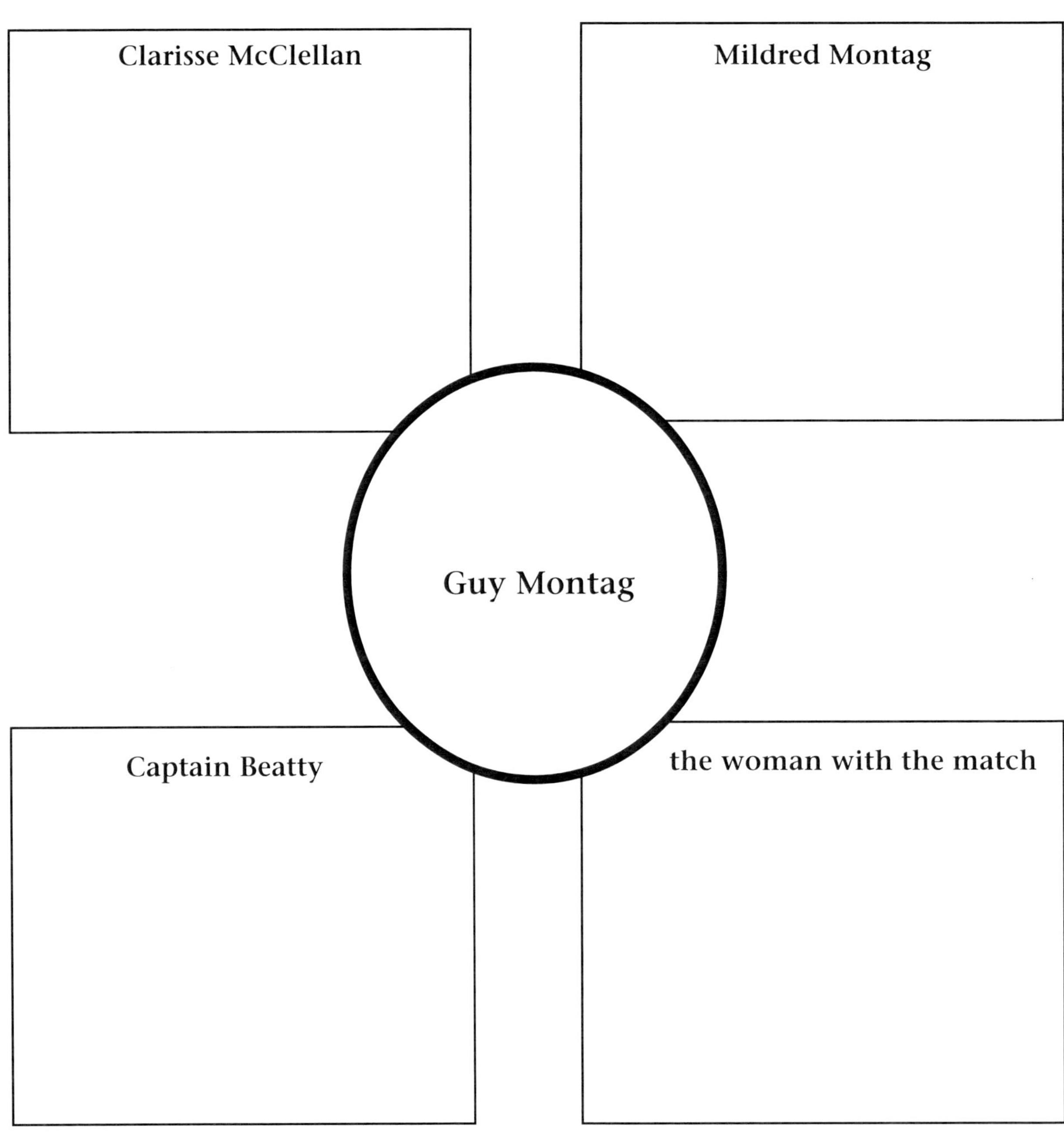

Name ______________________________

In Faber's Words

Directions: Faber gives Montag advice throughout the novel, often speaking in metaphors or using analogies to explain his ideas. Read each quote below, and explain in your own words what Faber is telling Montag.

Faber's Words	Explanation
1. "So now do you see why books are hated and feared? They show the pores in the face of life" (p. 79).	
2. "They're Caesar's praetorian guard, whispering as the parade roars down the avenue, 'Remember, Caesar, thou art mortal'" (p. 82).	
3. "Do your own bit of saving, and if you drown, at least die knowing you were headed for shore" (p. 82).	
4. "Our civilization is flinging itself to pieces. Stand back from the centrifuge" (p. 84).	
5. "Those who don't build must burn. It's as old as history and juvenile delinquents" (p. 85).	

Name ______________________________

Story Map

Directions: Complete the story map below for *Fahrenheit 451*.

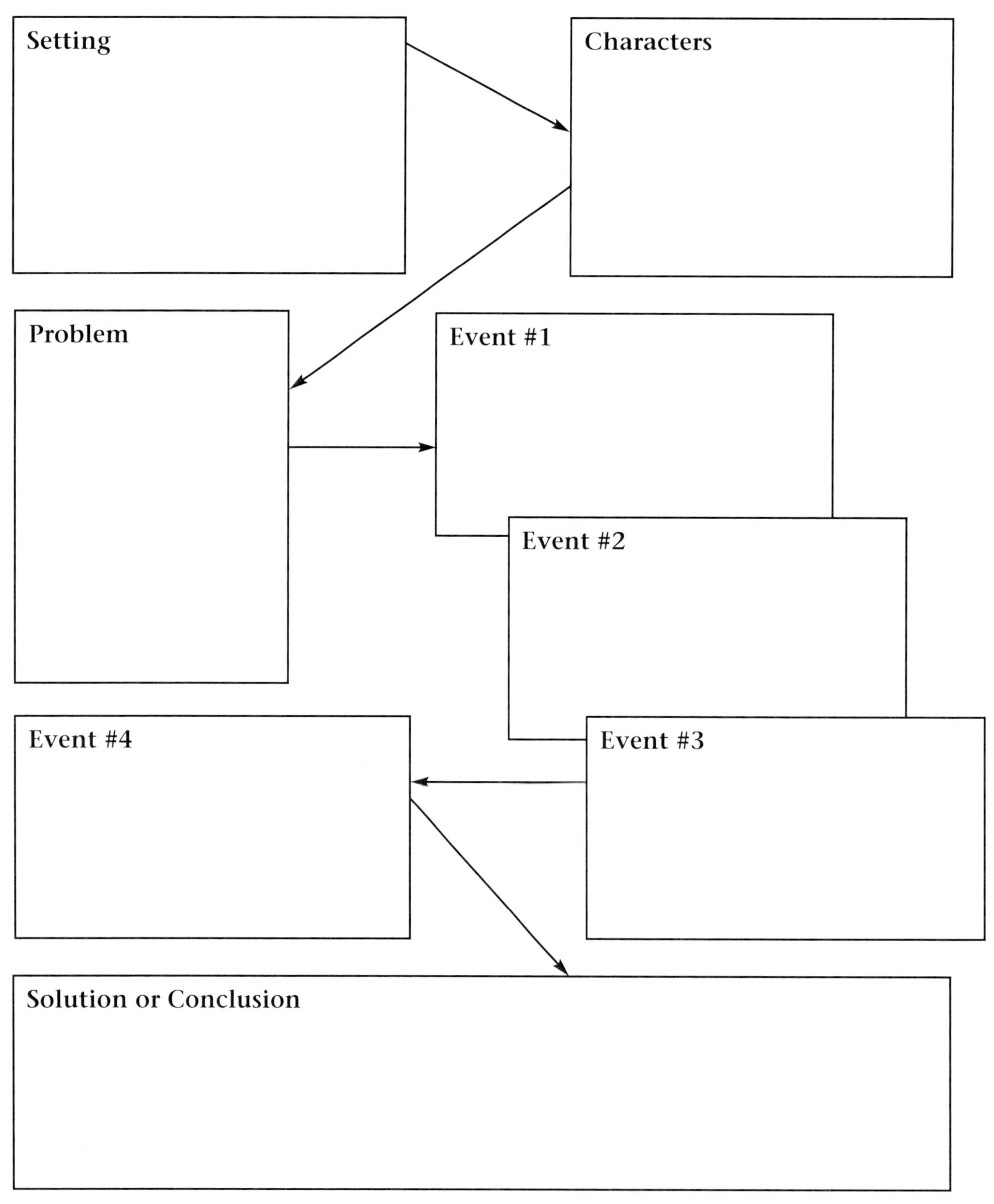

Name ______________________________

Symbolism

Directions: The story events listed below are more than simple actions. Each one symbolizes an element that is important to the underlying meaning of the novel. Write your explanation of the symbolism of each event.

1. Montag burns his own house, enjoying it somewhat.

____

____

____

2. Montag burns Beatty alive and later suspects that Beatty wanted to die.

____

____

____

3. The Hound manages to numb one of Montag's legs.

____

____

____

4. Montag hears on the radio that war has finally been declared.

____

____

____

5. Montag must cross a ten-lane highway and is almost killed by a car of joyriding children.

____

____

____

6. Montag leaves some books at the Blacks' home and then calls in an alarm.

____

____

____

Name ______________________________

Character Attribute Chart

Directions: Choose five characters from the novel. List their names in the first column. Fill in the other columns with the requested information.

Character	One-word Description	Appearance	Significance to the Story	Do you know anyone similar?

Name ______________________________

Burning Bright

The title of the third part of the novel is "Burning Bright." You may recognize these lines from William Blake's poem, "The Tyger." Study the first stanza.

Tyger! Tyger! burning bright
In the forests of the night,
What immortal hand or eye
Could frame thy fearful symmetry?

Directions: Relate these lines to Part Three of *Fahrenheit 451*.

1. In what way can Montag be seen as a tiger in the forests of the night?

____

____

____

____

2. What kind of "fearful symmetry" does Montag now have? (Think about how he used to be.) What symmetry lies in the rebuilding of the city?

____

____

____

____

3. What does "immortal" mean? What is immortal in *Fahrenheit 451*?

____

____

____

____

Name ______________________________

A New Montag

Directions: The Guy Montag at the beginning of the novel bears little resemblance to the Guy Montag who leads a group of intellectuals back to the city at the end of the novel. Trace his transformation by completing the activity below.

A. Montag at the Beginning

Write descriptive words and phrases.

1. ______________________________
2. ______________________________
3. ______________________________
4. ______________________________
5. ______________________________

B. Important Factors that Change Montag

Identify people and experiences.

1. ______________________________
2. ______________________________
3. ______________________________
4. ______________________________
5. ______________________________

C. Montag at the End

Write descriptive words and phrases.

1. ______________________________
2. ______________________________
3. ______________________________
4. ______________________________
5. ______________________________

Name ____________________________

Newspaper

Directions: Imagine you are part of the band of intellectuals left after the bombs are dropped on the city. Write a short account of what it is like trying to rebuild the city.

The Itinerant Eye

Wednesday, October 2 • Section A, Page 1

Name ______________________________

(Summarize Major Ideas)
A. Short Answer: Complete each sentence below.

1. The firemen in the novel are not what you'd expect because ____________________________

____

____.

2. Clarisse and her family are different from the other neighbors because they ______________

____

____.

3. Typical teenagers in the world of *Fahrenheit 451* amuse themselves by __________________

____

____.

B. Multiple Choice: Choose the BEST answer.

(Literary Devices)
____ 4. Why does Montag compare his role as a fireman to that of a symphony conductor?
   a. He feels the fire is his music and destroyed buildings are his masterpieces.
   b. He is authorized to order around civilians who come too near the fire site.
   c. He notices the other men work in unison and follow his lead at the fire site.
   d. He has been temporarily placed in charge of the men who work at his fire station.

(Cause/Effect)
____ 5. Why does Montag have to call emergency personnel for Mildred?
   a. Mildred fainted due to not eating or drinking enough.
   b. Mildred panicked when Montag began to read aloud to her.
   c. Mildred became unconscious after taking all of her sleeping pills.
   d. Mildred hyperventilated when Montag acted oddly in front of her friends.

(Inferences)
____ 6. Montag likely feels nervous around the Mechanical Hound because he has
   a. called in sick when he actually wasn't
   b. a secret stash of books stowed in his home
   c. had unpleasant encounters with the Hound before
   d. witnessed someone programming the Hound with his DNA

Name ______________________________

(Interpret Text)

____ 7. Why does Montag feel foolish for saying the words "once upon a time" to Beatty?
   a. The words reveal that Montag has read books.
   b. The words make Montag appear childish to his superior.
   c. He knows Beatty will correct any reference to literature he makes.
   d. He knows Beatty dislikes talking about the history of the firehouse.

(Main Idea and Details)

____ 8. What is rumored to have happened to Clarisse?
   a. She was arrested and jailed.
   b. She was hit by a car and killed.
   c. She overdosed on sleeping pills.
   d. She was shot and badly wounded.

(Inferences)

____ 9. Montag finally shows Mildred his stash of books because he
   a. thinks she will report him
   b. plans to frame her for the crime
   c. knows she will find out eventually
   d. feels she has a right to know about them

Name ______________________________

(Summarize Major Ideas)
A. Short Answer: Respond to each item below.

1. Why does Mildred prefer her "family" to the books Montag is reading aloud?

____

____

____

2. Describe Montag's trip on the subway to see Faber. What does he have with him? What does he try to do?

____

____

____

3. Explain how Beatty confuses Montag about books.

____

____

____

(Main Idea and Details)
B. True/False: Mark each with a *T* for true or an *F* for false.

____ 4. Montag calls Professor Faber once he realizes he needs a teacher.

____ 5. Faber insists that books are magical and their contents do not matter.

____ 6. Faber gives Montag a green device resembling a bullet that will help the two communicate.

____ 7. Montag reads an excerpt from *Gulliver's Travels* to Mildred and her friends.

____ 8. Mrs. Bowles bursts into tears after Montag reads aloud from a book.

____ 9. Mildred's friends voted for Winston Noble based on his name and appearance.

____ 10. On Montag's last fire call, the Salamander stops in front of Beatty's house.

Name ______________________________

(Summarize Major Ideas)
A. Short Answer: Respond to each item below.

1. To what mythological character does Beatty compare Montag, and why?

___

___

2. Why does Montag kill Beatty, and what does Montag theorize later about Beatty?

___

___

3. What part does the river play in Montag's escape?

___

___

4. Where does Montag run, and whom does he meet there?

___

___

(Interpret Text/Character Analysis)
B. Open-Ended Comprehension: Explain why Montag seems to enjoy burning his own home.

___

___

___

___

___

___

___

___

Name ______________________________

(Character Analysis)
A. Identification: Match each quote in the left column to the correct speaker in the right column.

____ 1. "I'm seventeen and I'm crazy."

____ 2. "Patience, Montag. Let the war turn off the 'families.'"

____ 3. "Why should I read? What *for*?"

____ 4. "Not everyone born free and equal, as the Constitution says, but everyone *made* equal."

____ 5. "Welcome back from the dead."

a. Faber
b. Granger
c. Clarisse
d. Mildred
e. Beatty

(Main Idea and Details)
B. True/False: Mark each with a *T* for true or an *F* for false.

____ 6. Clarisse is arrested for possession of books.

____ 7. Faber believes himself a terrible coward.

____ 8. Mildred is delighted to have Montag read poetry to her friends.

____ 9. Violence is an accepted form of entertainment in Montag's world.

____ 10. According to Beatty, Thomas Jefferson was the first fireman.

(Sequencing)
C. Sequencing: Using the letters *a–h*, put the following events in the order they occurred.

____ 11. Montag is forced to burn his own home and everything in it.

____ 12. The sounds and smells of nature nearly overwhelm Montag.

____ 13. Granger, Montag, and others seek to rebuild the demolished city.

____ 14. Mrs. Bowles and Mrs. Phelps storm out of the Montag residence.

____ 15. Montag watches a woman set her house, books, and herself aflame.

____ 16. Montag visits Faber's home to seek help interpreting literature.

____ 17. Beatty visits Montag's home to inquire about his health.

____ 18. Montag conceals books in a fellow fireman's home.

Name ______________________________

(Interpret Text)

D. Short Answer: Explain the significance of each section title from the novel.

19. The Hearth and the Salamander

____

____

20. The Sieve and the Sand

____

____

21. Burning Bright

____

____

(Literary Devices)

E. Figurative Language: Explain the comparison being made in each simile or metaphor below.

22. "[Montag felt Clarisse's] face was...like the dial of a small clock seen faintly in a dark room in the middle of a night [which] has to tell of the night passing swiftly on toward further darknesses, but moving also toward a new sun."

____

____

____

23. "I [Faber] remember the newspapers dying like huge moths. No one *wanted* them back. No one missed them."

____

____

____

Name ______________________________

24. "Now there was only the cold river and Montag floating...He felt as if he had left a stage behind and many actors."

____

____

____

F. Essay: Respond to two of the following on a separate sheet of paper.

(Literary Devices)

I. Choose one prominent symbol from the novel, and explain how that symbol ties in with the novel's themes, characters, and plot.

(Theme/Author's Purpose)

II. What message does the novel send about conformity versus individualism? Use specific examples from the novel to support your response.

(Character Analysis)

III. Discuss how each of Montag's three mentors/teachers (Clarisse, Faber, and Granger) contribute to his personal growth.

(Predictions)

IV. Make some predictions about the new society Montag, Granger, and the others intend to build. Be sure to emphasize how this new society will be different from the old one.

Answer Key

Activity #1: Answers will vary. Suggestions: adhering to convention, being obedient, maintaining traditional values, being orthodox, agreeing with the majority, the "bandwagon" mentality, complying with existing laws

Activity #2: 1. Ray Bradbury 2. Answers will vary. 3. 1953 4. 159 5.–6. Answers will vary.

Activity #3: A. 1. Both are related to the sense of smell. 2. Both have a luster or glow akin to gems. 3. Both relate to propulsion and projectiles. **B.** 4. tallow 5. minstrel 6. stratum 7. multifaceted 8. venomous 9. capillary 10. phoenix 11. stolid 12. cataract

Activity #4: Examples—Word #1: rollick; Clarisse refuses to *rollick* around town like other teenagers her age. Word #2: nomadic; Clarisse's family seems *nomadic,* often leaving one town for another. Word #3: breach; Montag cannot seem to *breach* Mildred's shallow outer veneer in order to speak to her about important things like books. Word #4: bestial; Montag begins to view his society, which shuns personal connection and past cultures, as *bestial.*

Activity #5: Example—Vocabulary Word: contemptible; Definition: worthy of scorn; Synonym: despicable; Antonym: noble; Pronunciation: kuhn-**temp**-tuh-buhl; Part of Speech: adjective; Sentence: The criminal's lack of remorse was *contemptible* to all assembled in the courtroom.

Activity #6: 1. overflowing 2. jealous 3. fashionable 4. loosened 5. shower 6. directed 7. inadequacy 8. protector 9. separate 10. stunning 11. deliberately 12. opaque 13. disrespectful 14. scorching

Activity #7:

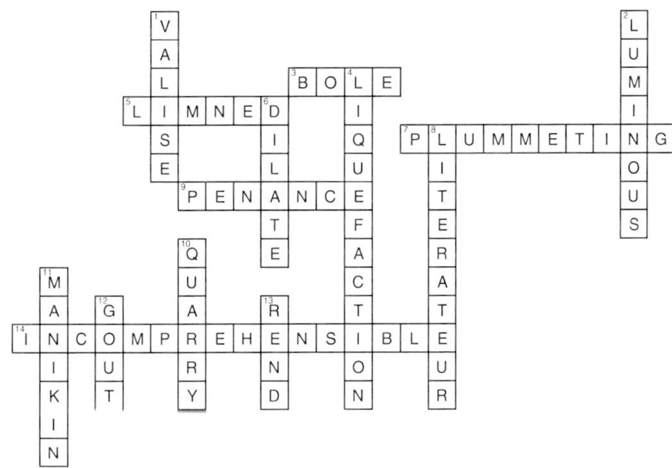

Activity #8: Examples—Word: juggernaut; Character: the Mechanical Hound; Explanation: The strength and speed of the Mechanical Hound make it a *juggernaut* among the humans in the novel. Word: squanders; Character: Montag; Explanation: Montag *squanders* much of his life by living in a society full of mindless fools. Word: desolation; Character: Faber; Explanation: Montag imagines that Faber left the city and is traveling through *desolation,* each destroyed city looking emptier than the next. Word: pyre; Character: Granger; Explanation: Granger believes a phoenix will rise from the *pyre* that is the burnt city.

Study Guide
Part One: The Hearth and the Salamander
Pages 1–29: 1. burning a house 2. He feels as if someone has been waiting there. 3. She has a slender, milk-white face, looks surprised and curious, has dark eyes, and is wearing a white dress. 4. reading books 5. "Are you happy" (p. 7)? 6. his bedroom 7. She overdosed on sleeping tablets.

8. One sucks out the contents of a person's stomach, and the other pumps all the blood from a person's body and replaces it with fresh blood and serum. 9. She watches three giant parlor screens. 10. that it tastes good 11. that he is not in love with anyone 12. the Mechanical Hound 13. because someone has programmed it that way 14. They kill each other.

Pages 29–66: 1. from a book of fairy tales he once burned 2. A woman is still in the house, and she burns the house and books herself. 3. the characters in the parlor shows Mildred watches 4. She says Clarisse was hit and killed by a car. 5. because his father and grandfather were firemen 6. to check on Montag, whom he heard was sick 7. "GUARANTEED: ONE MILLION LIGHTS IN THIS IGNITER" (p. 51) 8. They got increasingly shorter until they were no longer needed and were outlawed. 9. He is afraid of what will happen if Mildred pulls out his hidden book while Captain Beatty is there. 10. for people to be happy 11. drive their car into the country and hit animals at high speeds 12. numerous books 13. She is horrified and tries to burn the books. 14. that he doesn't like himself or any of the other firemen

Part Two: The Sieve and the Sand

Pages 67–88: 1. Clarisse 2. Montag shut it off. 3. Her friend calls her to talk about a parlor show. 4. because he needs a teacher 5. numb 6. a sieve and sand 7. the audio advertisements being played in the subway car 8. Montag stole and kept the Bible. 9. quality/texture, leisure to digest information, and the right to carry out actions based on the first two 10. the plan that he and Faber print extra books and hide them in firemen's houses so their homes will be burned 11. He begins ripping pages out of the Bible. 12. fiddling with electronics and radio transmissions 13. using the stock market 14. an earpiece that transmits and receives audio

Pages 88–106: 1. He feels that following someone blindly is no different than how he lived the first part of his life. 2. He will read to Montag while Montag is asleep. 3. turns off the parlor screens 4. The women discuss the candidates' appearances instead of any of their plans or policies. 5. He reads a poem. 6. Mildred has burned some of the books. 7. in the bushes in the backyard 8. a book 9. the majority 10. to Montag's house

Part Three: Burning Bright

Pages 107–133: 1. by sending the Mechanical Hound to Montag's house 2. It destroys responsibility and consequences. 3. The Mechanical Hound is in the neighborhood. 4. set fire to his own house 5. Mildred and her friends 6. to get the radio transmitter to fall out of his ear 7. burns them 8. that Beatty wanted to die 9. a news report designating Montag as a fugitive in the city 10. toward Faber's house 11. A beetle (car) nearly hits him. 12. They would have killed him for no reason. 13. Fireman Black's house; He leaves books in his kitchen so he can report the Blacks' house and it will be burned. 14. because he is finally doing the right thing and is not scared 15. Police have brought in a Mechanical Hound from another district. 16. burn everything he touched, wipe down surfaces with alcohol, turn the air conditioning on high, spray the rooms with moth spray, and turn on the lawn sprinklers 17. look out a door or window to see if they can spot Montag 18. He reaches the river, douses himself with whiskey, puts on Faber's old clothes, and lets himself be swept away by the current.

Pages 133–158: 1. in a barn loft by a quiet farmhouse 2. a deer 3. the railroad track 4. that Clarisse had walked on the same railroad track once 5. coffee and a colorless fluid that will change the chemical index of his perspiration 6. The police and the Hound kill another man so the public will think Montag paid for his crimes. 7. Fred Clement, former occupant of the Thomas Hardy chair at Cambridge; Dr. Simmons, a former specialist in Ortega y Gasset at U.C.L.A.; Professor West, a former ethics professor at Columbia University; and Reverend Padover, a former reverend 8. the Book of Ecclesiastes 9. because his grandfather would never be able to do the same amazing things again 10. A bomb is dropped, and the city is demolished. 11. to the city to rebuild it as a world that once again contains books and knowledge

Note: Answers for Activities #9–#18 will vary. Suggested answers are given where applicable.

Activity #9: Suggestions: burns books or reports those who have them, listens to authority, acts happy, uses and loves technology, is a consumer, refrains from meaningful relationships, is desensitized to violence, accepts things at face value

Activity #10: Example—Character: Faber; Conflict: Montag visits Faber's house, leaving a trail for the Mechanical Hound to follow; Resolution: Faber turns on sprinklers and cleans his house, erasing any trace of Montag's scent.

Activity #11: Suggestions—Clarisse McClellan questions everything Montag has always accepted as true. She sees him as a person and makes him think; Mildred Montag demonstrates to Montag how far humanity has slipped. Her dependence on pills and artificial entertainment to stay "happy" makes Montag yearn for something different; Captain Beatty quotes literary works to Montag, arousing Montag's interest in the way things used to be; The woman with the match is willing to die for her books, which further convinces Montag that there must be something worthwhile in them.

Activity #12: Suggestions—1. Books expose reality, something people often don't want to face. 2. Books remind us of our own mortality. 3. Do what you know is right, and at least you'll die knowing you did the best you could. 4. There is no need for destructive action, for society is destroying itself. 5. There are those who build and those who destroy; it's always been that way.

Activity #13: Setting—an unnamed future society; Characters—Guy Montag, Mildred Montag, Clarisse McClellan, Captain Beatty, the Mechanical Hound, Professor Faber; Problem—Montag becomes dissatisfied with the superficial society he lives in; Event #1—Montag hides books from the various sites the firemen are called to; Event #2—Montag visits Faber, who agrees to help him learn to comprehend literature; Event #3—Montag flees the city and joins a group of literateurs; Event #4—Montag's city is destroyed in a bombing; Solution or Conclusion—Montag and the group of intellectuals he met journey to the city to rebuild civilization.

Activity #14: Suggestions—1. Montag destroys his past life and ignorance with his home. 2. Beatty was unhappy in his life and knows being murdered is the only way he can die a "dignified" death. To die by burning is especially ironic. 3. Montag's injured leg holds him back, just as his society has done his entire life. 4. Montag's personal war, which has been building since the beginning of the novel, has also been officially "declared." He is a member of the resistance now. 5. The highway is like a gauntlet Montag must run in order to escape society. The absurdity of the situation is heightened by the children—horrible products of the society—trying to run him down. 6. This is Montag's first subversive act. He is getting his revenge on the society that has imprisoned him until this moment.

Activity #15: Example—Character: Mildred; One-word Description: mindless; Appearance: haggard; Significance to the Story: exemplifies the desensitized, consumer-driven society Montag and others live in; Answers will vary.

Activity #16: Suggestions: 1. Montag feels like an animal in the forest, drawn to the warmth of the fire built by the five men. 2. Whereas the old Montag was not real even to himself, the new, liberated Montag is not only real but whole and unashamed. Rebuilding the city is the final step in the triumph of those who value individual freedom and thought. The burners have destroyed themselves. The builders will rebuild but will remember at all times that they, too, are human and corruptible. 3. "Immortal" means "unable to die." In this novel, great ideas and great literature are immortal.

Activity #17: Suggestions—**A.** enjoys burning things, thinks only subconsciously about rebellion, feels his home is like a mausoleum, feels his wife is like a zombie, is not aware he is dissatisfied **B.** conversations with Clarisse, Clarisse's sudden disappearance, the woman burning alive with her books, meeting Faber, being turned in by Mildred and her friends **C.** happily burns down his own house, kills Beatty, becomes an enemy of society, meets the other runaways, finally understands the importance of literature

Activity #18: Answers will vary.

Quiz #1: A. 1. they start fires instead of putting them out 2. talk in the evening and have their own opinions; like to walk 3. smashing windows and cars at the Fun Park, racing cars on the roads, and shooting each other **B.** 4. a 5. c 6. b 7. a (p. 31) 8. b 9. d

Quiz #2: A. 1. Mildred is amused by the sensory aspects of her wall. She feels books offer her nothing. 2. Montag carries the Bible with him and tries to memorize the Book of Ecclesiastes amidst the torrent of audio advertisements being played on the subway. 3. Beatty quotes various writers who didn't agree about the nature of words and knowledge. **B.** 4. T 5. F 6. T 7. F 8. F 9. T 10. F

Quiz #3: A. 1. Icarus; Montag became overzealous about books just as Icarus did with flying. 2. Montag kills Beatty to protect Faber but later determines Beatty wanted to die. 3. The river carries Montag away from the city and hides his scent from the Hound. 4. Montag runs into the forest and meets other outcasts from society who have memorized entire literary works. **B.** Answers will vary. Suggestion—Many items in Montag's home remind him of how empty his life was before he met Clarisse and began really thinking. The beds likely remind him of his loveless marriage, Mildred's cosmetics chest likely reminds him of her superficiality, and the parlor likely reminds him of their utter lack of connection, especially in recent years. Now that Mildred has betrayed him by reporting his books, Montag is eager to destroy all evidence of the life he is leaving behind.

Novel Test: A. 1. c (p. 5) 2. a (p. 84) 3. d (p. 69) 4. e (p. 55) 5. b (p. 143) **B.** 6. F 7. T 8. F 9. T 10. F **C.** 11. e 12. g 13. h 14. d 15. a 16. c 17. b 18. f **D.** Answers will vary. Suggestions—19. A hearth traditionally symbolizes a home, and salamanders are portrayed in mythology as reptiles that are impervious to fire. Montag and his fellow firemen refer to the fire truck as the Salamander. Perhaps, at this point, the "hearth" is the fire station—a place where Montag feels comfortable. The firemen feel as if both can withstand fire, or are safe from harm. 20. When Montag first decides to begin reading the books he has stashed, he finds he cannot understand them. He compares the words tumbling through his mind to "a fierce whisper of hot sand through empty sieve" (p. 75). The words pour right through him, and his mind is left empty as a result. 21. In the third section of the novel, Montag is forced to burn his own home, which is "burning bright" once he is finished with it. Montag also burns Beatty to death in this section. The section title may also refer to Montag's mind, which is "burning bright" with knowledge, questions, and the will to rebuild a society that has been demolished. Students might also make connections between this section of the novel and William Blake's poem, "The Tyger." **E.** Answers will vary. Suggestions—22. Montag feels Clarisse is an indication of a very different era, or "new sun," on the horizon for the world (p. 8). 23. Faber recalls when newspapers were abruptly eliminated, "fluttering" to their metaphoric death as people became disinterested in reading them (p. 85). 24. Montag finally feels he can be himself rather than playing a part, as he did in his old life (p. 133). **F.** Essays will vary. Refer to the scoring rubric on page 35 of this guide.

Linking Novel Units® Student Packets to National and State Reading Assessments

During the past several years, an increasing number of students have faced some form of state-mandated competency testing in reading. Many states now administer state-developed assessments to measure the skills and knowledge emphasized in their particular reading curriculum. This Novel Units® guide includes open-ended comprehension questions that correlate with state-mandated reading assessments. The rubric below provides important information for evaluating responses to open-ended comprehension questions. Teachers may also use scoring rubrics provided for their own state's competency test.

Scoring Rubric for Open-Ended Items

3-Exemplary	Thorough, complete ideas/information Clear organization throughout Logical reasoning/conclusions Thorough understanding of reading task Accurate, complete response
2-Sufficient	Many relevant ideas/pieces of information Clear organization throughout most of response Minor problems in logical reasoning/conclusions General understanding of reading task Generally accurate and complete response
1-Partially Sufficient	Minimally relevant ideas/information Obvious gaps in organization Obvious problems in logical reasoning/conclusions Minimal understanding of reading task Inaccuracies/incomplete response
0-Insufficient	Irrelevant ideas/information No coherent organization Major problems in logical reasoning/conclusions Little or no understanding of reading task Generally inaccurate/incomplete response

Notes